My Science Library

D0792905

Why Plants Become Extinct

by Julie K. Lundgren

Science Content Editor:
Shirley Duke

Rourke
Educational Media

rourkeeducationalmedia.com

Scan for Related Titles
and Teacher Resources

Science Content Editor: Shirley Duke holds a bachelor's degree in biology and a master's degree in education from Austin College in Sherman, Texas. She taught science in Texas at all levels for twenty-five years before starting to write for children. Her science books include *You Can't Wear These Genes, Infections, Infestations, and Diseases, Enterprise STEM, Forces and Motion at Work, Environmental Disasters*, and *Gases*. She continues writing science books and also works as a science content editor.

www.rourkeeducationalmedia.com

Project Assistance: The author thanks the staff at Como Zoo Conservatory for orchid rescue information.

Photo credits: Cover © Galyna Andrushko, basel101658; Table of Contents © J.K. York; Page 4 © Woudloper name: Sphenophyllum_miravallis; Page 4/5 © Christopher Meder - Photography; Page 6 © skvoor; Page 6/7 © Stéphane Bidouze; Page 8 © John Charles Meliss; Page 8/9 © basel101658; Page 10 © Chapelle; Page 11 © J.K. York; Page 12 © Mikhail Melnikov; Page 12/13 © Brykaylo Yuriy; Page 14 © JeremiahsCPs name: Kinabalu_Mesilau_N._rajah_upper_pitcher_3; Page 15 © AridOcean, Todd Boland; Page 16 © zirconicusso; Page 17 © fotokik_dot_com; Page 18 © Terric Delayn; Page 18/19 © U.S. Fish and Wildlife Service; Page 20 © Kamira; Page 20/21 © Colin D. Young;

Editor: Kelli Hicks

My Science Library series produced by Blue Door Publishing, Florida for Rourke Educational Media.

Library of Congress PCN Data

Lundgren, Julie K.
 Why Plants Become Extinct / Julie K. Lundgren.
 ISBN 978-1-61810-089-4 (Hard cover) (alk. paper)
 ISBN 978-1-61810-222-5 (Soft cover)
 Library of Congress Control Number: 2012930292

Rourke Educational Media
Printed in the United States of America,
North Mankato, Minnesota

Also Available as:

rourkeeducationalmedia.com

customerservice@rourkeeducationalmedia.com
PO Box 643328 Vero Beach, Florida 32964

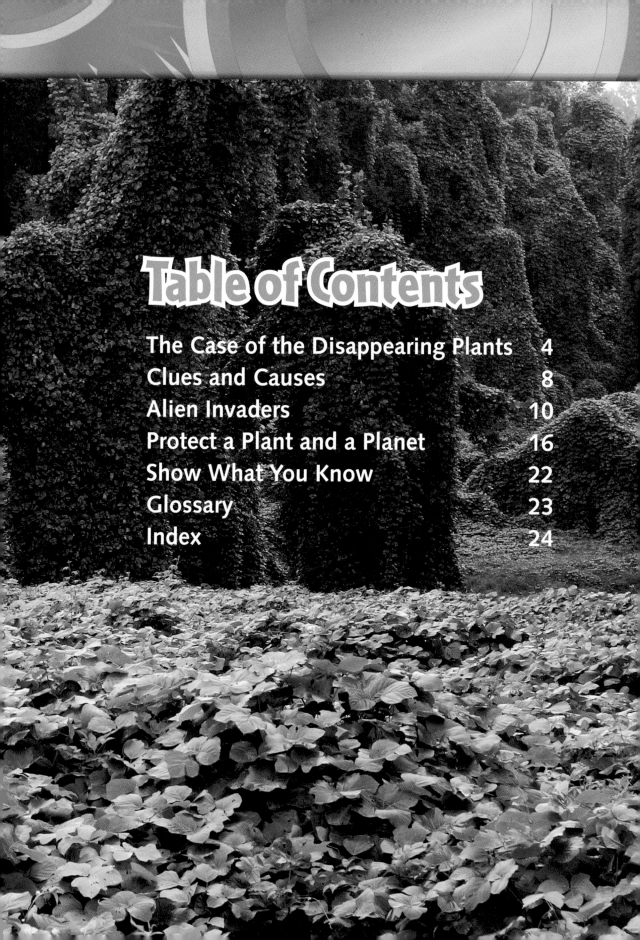

Table of Contents

The Case of the Disappearing Plants

Calling all detectives! Plants everywhere have gone missing. **Extinction** threatens many others. **Habitats** containing hundreds of plants found nowhere else on Earth face danger, particularly plants in rainforests, on islands, and along shorelines. One in five of Earth's plant **species** is at risk of extinction.

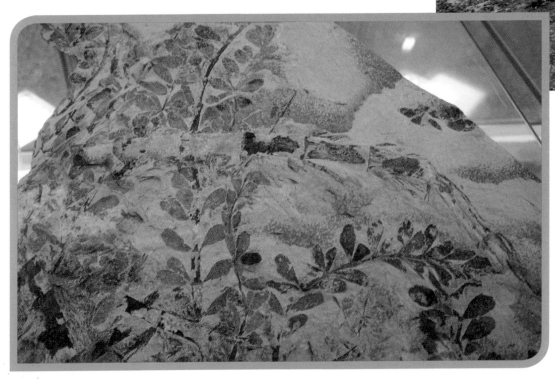

Plant fossils give scientists clues about what Earth's climate was like when the plants lived.

The overall increase in Earth's temperature causes ocean water levels to rise, flooding shoreline plants.

Throughout Earth's history, plant extinctions have happened as a natural part of a changing planet. Vast seas containing prehistoric saltwater plant life once covered most of central North America where grasslands and forests now grow. As Earth's land and **climate** changed over millions of years, plants changed, too. They developed new ways to reproduce, take in **nutrients**, and gather sunlight more efficiently.

Slow habitat changes give plants time to develop new **adaptations**. Recent changes have happened much too quickly for many plants to adapt.

We depend on plants for food and oxygen. We use plants for fuel, building materials, and medicine.

RED ALERT! We need to solve the mystery of the disappearing plants quickly before more become extinct.

The bark of the rare Florida yew, a tree found only along a short stretch of a single river in northwestern Florida, contains an ingredient that may fight cancer. When plant species disappear, we lose their special ingredients.

The trees and plants of the rainforest take in large amounts of carbon dioxide and give off oxygen, helping Earth's climate remain stable.

Clues and Causes

Ecologists, the scientists who study the connections between plants, animals, and the places they live, study changes in the populations of living things. They have identified several main reasons for plant losses, all caused by people.

Found only on the island of St. Helena, the St. Helena olive tree became extinct because of deforestation and overgrazing by cattle.

Deforestation, or the widespread practice of harvesting a forest without replanting, occurred frequently in early America. Today's deforestation more often occurs in places like tropical rainforests.

The number of people on Earth increases each year. People remove forests and grasslands for farming and for timber to meet increasing human needs. Deforestation and overgrazing by cattle cause major plant habitat loss.

Alien Invaders

People sometimes bring plants from one place to another. **Native** species cannot compete against these alien invaders.

Case Study 1

Americans introduced purple loosestrife, a European species, into their gardens. Seeds from this plant easily wash into rivers and lakes where it crowds out native plants and clogs waterways.

The worst invaders grow quickly, spread easily, and grow well in many habitats, killing many native species in the process.

Case Study 2

In 1876, farmers began growing Japanese kudzu as possible food for cattle. The vines now cloak forests in the southeastern United States, blocking sunlight from native plants.

Sometimes a decline in one species endangers another species. **Endangered** prairie fringed **orchids** rely on hawk moths for pollination. **Pesticides** and pollution threaten hawk moths, causing their populations to decline.

The loss of hawk moths makes the orchids' future uncertain.

Global climate change affects habitats and plant survival. Coastal areas containing rare plants may flood due to rising oceans.

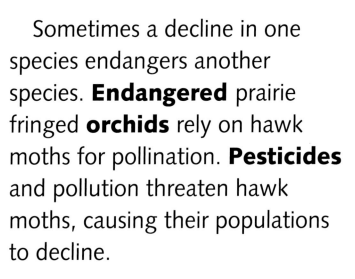

United States

Temperate Forest

Temperate Grassland   Alpine

Northern Coniferous
Forest   Arid Land

Conifer forests grow better in cooler temperatures in the United States, but temperate forests and grasslands push these pine forests north as seasonal temperatures warm.

**Nepenthes rajah
pitcher plant**

Poachers collect
and sell endangered
carnivorous plants.

Plant collectors contribute to the decline of some plants. In Burma, a country in southeast Asia, people steal rare orchids from the wild to sell. Because of this, Burma's forests no longer contain rainbow orchids.

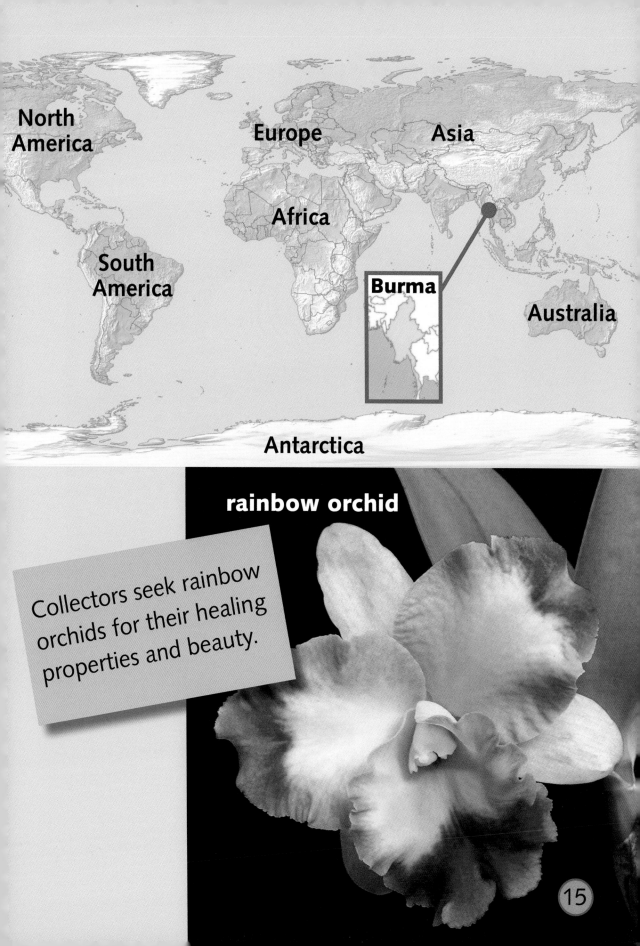

North
America

Europe

Asia

Africa

South
America

Burma

Australia

Antarctica

rainbow orchid

Collectors seek rainbow orchids for their healing properties and beauty.

Protect a Plant and a Planet

Lady's Slipper Orchid

The U.S. Fish and Wildlife Service catches plant smugglers taking plants like rare orchids. They send captured plants to rescue teams who have places and skills to care for the plants. Even with care, many rescued plants die.

Countries may save special habitats as parks. In the United States, western national parks protect some of the lands where giant redwoods grow.

South America

Chile

In 2011, Chile created a new national park to protect endangered alerces trees. Before this, loggers could cut down as many of these conifers as they wished.

Rescue sites like the Como Zoo Conservatory in St. Paul, Minnesota, take in smuggled plants, care for them, and seek to return them to their home countries.

You can join a group to help save endangered plants. Volunteers in Illinois have worked successfully to help the fringed prairie orchid in their state. They plant seeds, pollinate flowers by hand, manage habitats, and count these plants yearly.

Instead of leaving it to Mother Nature, people increase the chance of successful plant reproduction by pollinating flowers by hand. Using a fine paintbrush, they transfer pollen from one flower to another.

Landowners concerned about the prairie fringed orchid have set aside land for habitat protection.

People need to farm, build houses, and harvest trees, but we must learn to keep these activities in balance with the needs of plants and their natural habitats. We also need to investigate whenever native plants begin to disappear. Solving the case could save a plant species from extinction!

With so many plants in danger, we cannot wait. Every person and country must work together to protect Earth's **biodiversity**. Learn about endangered plants and habitats in your area. Understand what causes plants to die out. Tell others what you have learned.

Write a letter to government officials explaining your concerns about endangered plants in your state. They may be able to help you raise awareness about this important issue.

As people create manmade beaches and build houses, hotels, and other shoreline developments, natural habitats change. Plants like the dwarf lake iris become threatened.

Show What You Know

1. Name some causes of plant extinction.

2. How do nonnative plants contribute to the loss of native plants?

3. What can we do to protect endangered plants?

Glossary

adaptations (ad-ap-TAY-shunz): ways groups of animals change over time to help them survive, including changes in the way they look and act

biodiversity (bye-oh-duh-VUR-suh-tee): the condition of nature in which a wide variety of species live in a single area

climate (KLYE-mit): the usual temperature, rain, or snowfall, and weather in a place

endangered (en-DAYN-jerd): at risk of becoming extinct

extinction (ek-STINGKT-shun): the complete loss of a species of plant or animal from the Earth

habitats (HAB-uh-tats): homes for living things where they can find everything they need to live, including food and shelter

native (NAY-tiv): naturally occurring, living in the place where it originated

nutrients (NOO-tree-uhnts): things needed for healthy growth, like vitamins and minerals

orchids (OR-kidz): a group of plants, often collected and grown for their showy and unusual flowers

pesticides (PESS-tuh-sydz): chemicals used to kill insects harmful to people or crops

species (SPEE-sheez): a category or kind of organism grouped together by their shared traits

Index

Websites to Visit

www.ecokids.ca/pub/kids_home.cfm

www.globio.org/glossopedia/article.aspx?art_id=20&art_nm=Conservation

www.mbgnet.net/sets/rforest/index.htm

About the Author

Julie K. Lundgren has written more than 40 nonfiction books for children. She gets a kick out of sharing juicy facts about science, nature, and animals, especially if they are slightly disgusting! Through her work, she hopes kids will learn that Earth is an amazing place and young people can make a big difference in keeping our planet healthy. She lives in Minnesota with her family.

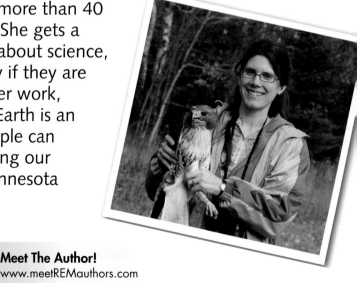

Meet The Author!
www.meetREMauthors.com